ashes are bone and dust

Also by the author

Hard Candy

ashes are bone and dust

poems by Jill Battson

INSOMNIAC PRESS

Edited by Mike O'Connor
Copy edited by Catherine Jenkins
Designed by Mike O'Connor

National Library of Canada Cataloguing in Publication Data

Battson, Jill
    Ashes are bone and dust

Poems.
ISBN 1-894663-04-7

I. Title.

PS8553.A8336A83 2001   C811'.54   C2001-930394-7
PR9199.3.B37A83 2001

The publisher gratefully acknowledges the support of the Canada
Council, the Ontario Arts Council and Department of Canadian
Heritage through the Book Publishing Industry Development
Program.

Printed and bound in Canada

Insomniac Press, 192 Spadina Avenue, Suite 403,
Toronto, Ontario, Canada, M5T 2C2
www.insomniacpress.com

THE CANADA COUNCIL | LE CONSEIL DES ARTS
FOR THE ARTS | DU CANADA
SINCE 1957 | DEPUIS 1957

ONTARIO ARTS COUNCIL
CONSEIL DES ARTS DE L'ONTARIO

this book is dedicated to the two people I never
thought I'd have to live without

my parents
Joyce and Tom
(1924/22 - 1997)

without death there is no history

I want to thank the usual cast of characters for their unending support: AM Allcott; Mark Breslin; Waheeda Harris; Adeena Karasick; Mike O'Connor and James Spyker – I hope they know how important they are.
Thanks to John Armstrong who helped me focus again, Catherine Jenkins for her laser eyeballs, my great new friend Bill Arms and not forgetting Witkin, the green eyed, grey thing that takes over most of the bed.
Thanks also to the funding bodies and their panels who deemed my writing worthy of support:
The Toronto Arts Council; The Ontario Arts Council and The Canada Council.

And most of all thanks to my sister, Ann, a newly discovered friend, wonderful companion and great supporter.

Ancient History

Cold as the breeze foretelling autumn
a chill through bones, deaf message
when fingers lightly trace the history of marriage
along blue lines the colour of regret
a sign of memory in night's clarity
the ceiling offers no comfort
solitude is the salt-slick skin offered to a milky moon.

Really Dead This Time

for Ian

When another poet recites your words
I remember I haven't seen you in a year
later I take down your book from the shelf
because I want to borrow your words for my poem
        really dead this time
and my name glares back from the page of acknowledgements
admonishing me for not seeing it when you were alive
you are the last death I could care about
raw edge of the buildup
there are voids where I never think about you
days when I play your image in my mind
eternally, internally
in the smallest places
I saw you in the year-end obit in Xtra!
shocked to see you where I knew you'd be
the card at Christmas from your lover
emptiness between lines of normality
I miss you too
déja vu of you sitting silent at the Rivoli, bone-sore
smoking dope by candlelight in our spare room
to relieve the nausea
and the book you bought me is always on the coffee table
your dedication a berserk spider crawl
I kept every letter you sent me with their stamps from the '60s
envelopes alive with stickers and scrawl
remembering the disease, it gave me you
two years before and you are
        really dead this time.

Suspension While Moving

Running away from you, from the coast
from the hundreds of miles of sea separating us
suspended slosh of coffee, the stomach seizes
over white table linen
I am running toward your voice, toward hope
and every cold phone receiver pushed against my ear
in the sleeting afternoon
icy tarmac of each highway rest stop
tells me nothing of time
just the suspension of all things
a chance to hear your voice again, once more, at all
running toward hope, past greasy burger stands
the winter-bare standing maples
rutted flashing fields of dried cornstalks
in the calm soft car interior, outside rush of destiny
suspension while moving
running scared against the irony of distance
I am running away from you, toward your voice.

Discomfort

It is in the sleeting winter
when the trees are bare-boned spirits to spring
that I am lye-eyed with shock and cold
each heavy crystal formation warms into cold glass
I look upon the wind as if it were solid
a sheet of cold penetrating my being
in the sleeting winter she died.

It is in the steaming summer
when the dense city heat threatens to bust open skulls
sidewalks tremble and blister breathing
and I am dull and heavy with smothering heat
verdant leaf burden, the laden trees
pitch wearily under hopeful hot breeze
in the steaming summer he died.

Sanguine

One

And the way it enters the body
a dull puncture into the surprise of flesh
never feeling the insert in adrenalin overdrive
blackness rushing in
I will never know what happened to part of my life
that early morning
popular time for exits
that morning when I lost the beginning of me
the humours are substances that leave the body
first it is blood
a trickle, a spurt, a pooling, a pulse
or when in trauma
globules of a person's essential fluid
explode on impact — even the tiniest of drops
and rush out in a small soaking of fabric
touching all people in the vicinity
a doctor sluices it off his gloves
whirlpool crimson of life into the drain
from body to sink in three minutes
a nurse looks into her bathroom mirror
on returning home hours later
scratches a flea-sized spot of blood from her cheek
and parts of my beginning travel abroad, separately
at different times, in various forms
or dull to brown, cooling, coagulating
but all is lost.

Two

Because we are usually placed on our backs
when we die
the body relaxes itself to gravity
shifting, settling
a million revolutions to the centre of the earth
o planet
and when she sees the corpse in the afternoon
of that same day
seemingly months have rolled out in seconds
a heartbeat that changes all time
the future and her place in it
altered in ways which will never be clear
there is still a trauma in the expression of the face
etched but softening
falling, falling, shifting and settling
lifesaving measures — civilized oddity
puncture in the neck
pulling open like a small, second vulva
purple and bloody within its fold.

The Dress

Surprisingly small collection of clothes inside my mother's wardrobe
I am puzzled at their shabbiness
necks slightly frayed, florals muted
her particular perfume enclosed, mixing lavendar/camphor
cardigans and dresses, smaller than I remember
indigo, sky, pale, navy and all other shades of blue
I picked a dress to bury her in
bright, animated, full of life
for the rest of the clothes I had to call the Salvation Army.

At Austin's Funeral Home

I'm holding tight to my hands,
lest they shake like a dose of Parkinson's
white and numb with the experience
the funeral home curtains are heavy with collected grief
a silent carpet cushions us, every fibre waiting
the air gives the impression of something solid
as if each dust mote hangs suspended
        a rolling ball of microscopic woven dimension
anticipating a foot to fall
a fainting body to thump the ground
a sob to roll crescendo from the throat
the door opens and I realize in a second
that my life, extended
will never clash with this one again
        if lives are a singular column of energy
        bound to impact on others

I don't remember if moonlight came through
the bedroom windows of our house
shone on us while we slept and made us mad
with the silver every month
but I remember her asleep in the bed
washed by the blues of a street light
the way it curved indigo through her hair
sweet shush of a midnight car on flaccid streets
the slight click at the back of her throat
there are remembrances in that room
sighing over me with the breeze
of my many years in the house
from doilies on bedside tables, mints in a glass jar

chalky with promise of peppermint
dual clocks, their heartbeats a regular comfort
telling the different times of ordinary people
there is a sleepiness, peaceful and summer-warm
faint fragrance of lawns and primroses
drifting through open windows
suspension that feels like childhood, or love, or beauty
as if I could stay in that room forever
and remember our lives as they should have been
and she is alive there, even in the cotton rustle of sleep
the darkness of my memory

and in the corridors of the funeral home
there is a suspension that feels like death, or surprise,
or anticipation
emotions triggered as my heart leaps
pounding into upper chest
I wish I could be dead instead of having to deal with it
framed by the door
the coffin is the same height as my parents' bed
she is lying there as if asleep
like the thousand nights I have watched her
as a child, as a teenager, as a woman
standing beside her marriage bed
breathed her breath
as in the womb where my history began with her
double breath, life-sustaining breath
the coffin's sentinel lid watching upright from the corner
ash wood, fault lines of orange shot through blond grain
breath catches in a tightening body as I step into the room
it contains no energy, no soul, no life
dead like a sound booth

and she is smaller than I remember
the wood lined with white satin
a lace cloth partially hiding her mottled, bare blue feet
bruised hands clasping each other
her face looks exactly like in life, in sleep
but when I touch her she is cold and I am terrified
silence crashes through the room, my eyes will not shut
a deafening roar inside my brain
I am panicked, contained, hysterical
the musky odor of the dead, scent of freesias
my memory overwritten with the horrible image of her neck
crushed into her shoulders, like nothing living
I cannot stand this image of my mother
soul, energy, life flown out of her in a second after failure
and in this moment which I thought would last for hours
I turn and push everything out of my way
panic to escape my senses working in high gear
the smell, the silence, the cold flesh, the panic
rushing through the corridors of Austin's funeral home.

Neck

Seven folds, orange pink softness
strata that fold along a base, overlap and intertwine
pushing against collagen, a variance of strength
circle of remembrance, knowledge
holding to a lifetime of belief
     soft down of powdered fragrance
nibbling centre of affection
the luminescent glow of life, flat in death
condensing of grief into shoulders
the atlas condition as weight falls into the world
into death
     flesh relaxes to gravity
vertebrae open, a life of pressure
released from the flattened sponge within
relaxing, stiffening, relaxing
     seven folds separating body from head
median between mind and function
passage interruptus
heart muscle interruptus
the attitude of death.

Identifying Death's Perfume

Scuffing up the wool twill smell of carpet
releasing dry dust — thin coating over teeth
swish of nylon, warmed flesh frictions
swang of lemon furniture polish tangs the air
quick twist brings perfume of shampoo off heated scalp
          vacuum air rush as the door opens
triggers primal brain's catalogue
too far back and away to remember
twitching backload brings it into focus
selecting, sorting the smells
musky odour, manifests on the tongue like distress, like blood
sweet custard freesias
blossom of decay
forever linking memory/fragrance/emotion.

Her Hands

They say that skin feels waxy in death
and it does
and also cold
not wet/icy like chicken from the refrigerator
but cooler than living flesh
when hands are cold to the touch
from winter weather
there is still the thread of life coursing beneath
promising warmth
not the dull layers
that make up the tissues of death.

Rose Detail in Green Daylight

A thumbtack of thickened paint here
shiny, almost wet
red
the mouths of wartime women
a rose in its attitude of the tribal
paint layer upon layer
      by knocking the edge of raw pastry with a blunt knife
      we make it flaky, tectonic
as oil paint worked on glass
opacity of the ages
my mother built lipsticks
in the warm blue kitchen of our '50s childhood
from the necessity of making ends meet
circular housekeeping
scraping out the unswivelable ends from their metal casings
melting together the crimson wax slowly
like liquid chocolate to sculpt Valentine's Day roses
mother's mouth smell of red, of gloss
a kissable melt in a white porcelain bowl over boiling water
blood and roses, life and death
and pouring it back into a solitary tube
      on cooling the lipstick, twirled up,
      had the geographic complexity
      of smooshed lava, contained clay
or red oil paint
layered by knife onto a surface that gives good structure
hers was the frugality of economy
a thin layer of red accentuating the cushiony sensual
the paint, a gesture of abundance
endless metal tube of pigmented oil

extravagance built up onto the surface
closeted acid wax aroma tang
offerings that were both gorgeous and spiteful.

Three Times in Our Lives

for Sid

One. at six weeks, you held me to your worsted chest
wind blowing softly across hillside above an open grave
the cemetery, August flowers
our flesh is being buried

Two. at thirty-seven years, your warm hard palm against mine
clouds scudding across sometimes blue high sky
the street, April chill
my flesh is being buried

Three. at thirty-seven years, you clasped me
to your polyester chest
damp with summer breeze and moisture
the last day in our house, June humidity
our flesh is being buried.

Floral Tribute

The French create porcelain roses for their graves
beauty for an eternity
in the crowded cemeteries of Père Lachaise and Montparnasse
among celebrity dead and common folk
angels and naked women soar to the grey Parisian heavens
let us in, let us in
cherubs weep on marble sarcophagi
draped figures peek from doorways
girls in Grecian gowns throw themselves face down on tombs
there is a chaos of suffering sculpted here
monuments reaching up in a rush to a sky
which drops acid rain and soot as penance
bowers of ancient trees shade
white gravel borders slivers of green and grey stone
and between the carved shadows serene porcelain flowers glow
with otherworldly colour and glaze
a special hope in the canyons of eternal repose.

A Visitor Named Memory

When Uncle Sid sat with him
after a fifteen year absence
my father kept his eyes on the floor,
his trouser leg, his clasped hands
and although, at other times, he was mostly incoherent
jived with Sid like the two shared a mind
like the two were living back in 1932
in the sun-heavy kitchen of their Horningsham cottage
clear as a bell, my father remembered
Sid pushing him off a stool
that stolen raspberry pie
their mother's stiff white apron
her hard jaw
and the two of them finishing each other's sentences
in a lightning boyhood closeness
smells, visions, light and dark
a fluorescence of colour coming to me
as if I were sharing those memories also
kinetic too strong to take breath
and him never once looking at Sid
as if he were talking to memories
a ghostly image of his former life
or maybe he was afraid of bursting into tears of recognition
or of the imminence of the end.

Last Days

Those last days with my father
for the most part, had the feeling of Sunday afternoons
at our house when we still played card games
and put the pieces in country cottage puzzles
serene and passive,
blue-toned with coal smoke and filtered sunlight
lulling to The Clitheroe Kid and The Archers on the wireless

Immersed in this institution's old urine smell
we are cocooned in memories
a time before stress
stroking his fingers the length of my arm
lingering, squeezing his hand over the back of mine
moments stringing out across hours of timelessness
watery sun shifting across an audience of empty vinyl chairs
ochre, green, burgundy
in a television room too hot
we wing-backed against the blare of talk shows
speaking underneath the cartoon-character squeal

In a place marked by mealtimes
we face the crowded pandemonium
of a cabbage-scented dining room
where I slice chicken into dignity morsels
for him to feed himself
his perfect table manners not designed for disjunctiveness
brain shifting ideas of likes and dislikes
of images and words
accompanied by the sobbing of an inmate
subsumed by Parkinson's jerks
we breath in the hell of institutions

And in the afternoon when we are alone, knee-to-knee
his touch light and familiar on my hand
he explains why Aldwych station is closed
or what happened during liberation
his once long, manicured nails
uneven and catching the light in a Halloween raggedness
broken and cracked from crawling along the floor
to pick up imaginary kittens and babies
he shapes the air with his fingers' hard strength
and touches my face with this taut skin
as gentle as love.

Hierarchy

Pushing the hotel room door open
the place is changed
its space physically waits for me, holding its breath
    a figure could move away from the curtains
    hands clasped behind its back in an attitude of waiting
    someone could lift themselves slowly from the bed
    reality unblurring itself, leaving covers dented and warm
        and I wouldn't be surprised
everything seems on hold in the heavy southern atmosphere
phone light blinks into the fabric-inspired twilight of the room
red focus of the space, pulsing, reflecting in polished veneer
    the light, blinks, red
for a time I sit on the bed watching its metronomic beat
my jacket still crooked over the inside of my elbow
palm anchors me to the counterpane
my face muscles droop
the Atlanta sultry heat somehow settles
through the air conditioning
light moves from white to yellow
shadows pass along the wall
    I am damp
I pick up the message to hear my sister
her cracked voice a transatlantic, trans-America siren
sparking my fears
we are both too far from home, from family
our agreement is that she doesn't phone
unless something happens to our father
now she is unreachable in the rainy barrenness of north Wales
and I know nothing

Afternoon passes into evening
stretches out, a humid gloaming
lush vegetation, a promise of smothering beyond windows
porters whistle cabs five floors down
yellow light turns orange, then blue
scent of roses and chlorine
the office building across the street shuts off its lights
    is he sicker?
    is he dead?
I watch hotel movies,
drink the dry sharpness of mediocre hotel wine
eat cheesies
oral comfort on my orange fingers
try to feel the answer in commercial breaks
to feel his essence between the cathode rays;
the thousand souls in this hotel

In the morning, light reverses itself blue to yellow
I lie awake for hours in the dry-eyed gasping deadened
stillness of the room
listening to the small sounds that signal others are rising
flush of water like a small storm
doors popping closed in the corridor
the maid calling out good morning
jingling her all-access key chain
stagnant air night breath hangs in the room
overturned glass stains red
on white rose print embossed damask napkin
a silver tray
junk food packages from the vending machine
scrunched out of desirability scatter the bedside table
at 7 a.m. the phone shrills

it is her
he is dead
I move up in the hierarchy of our family.

Mixing Ashes

On the afternoon before my parents' wedding anniversary I walk to the village. A windblown day with a blue velvet canopy. Warm February. I go to the hardware store to buy a clean bucket. I ask for a bucket with a lid, but they are all out. The one I purchase stares up at me with an idiot question. The plastic grey, speckled. A bird's eggshell cylinder mural. I wanted a new bucket. Not one already existing in the household, sullied by minute traces of potato peelings, earth, the carrot and bile chunkiness of vomit. I want the sterile sharpness of bone fragments clean. Fresh in their newness. Nothing mingling. On this day fifty-five years ago the hoarfrost would be down. Winters being colder then. The same sky. The same blue. Stomachs fluttering with the anticipation of individual lives linking. My father pressing his RAF uniform. My mother fingering eau-de-nil silk. The felt black cat with the silver horseshoes and bells. In a moment on earth I think all of this. It is only eight months and still my emotions are skin peeled outwards. Raw skin with a wool cardigan drawn over it. It is hard to be alone in grief.

In the utility room at my sister's house I lay out the utensils on the chest freezer that has become my workbench. The bucket is there. The freezer's white, minutely pocked surface questions me. This room is overlooked by the studio windows from where, at three o'clock in the afternoon, I see my sister working. I wipe the surface clean. Take two identical dark grey plastic canisters from their cardboard sarcophagi. Place one on the left, one on the right. So I will remember who is who. Twist the lids off and lay their contents bare. Inside are plastic liners. Inside the plastic liners are the ashes of my parents. On the left my father is heavier than my mother, his ashes lighter in colour. On the right my mother crumbles, considering.

I've found two new glass spice jars with vacuum lids in the pantry. In each one I measure a teaspoon of each parent and mix together. The most careful action I have executed in months. A jar for my sister, a jar for me. Fragment reminder of their bodies, tangency of souls. Like a Victorian hair broach, twisted locks of the dead surrounded by jet. Polished lignite of this country.

Turning my attention to the bucket I pour a small and equal amount from each canister into its emptiness. Mix with a wooden spoon. Carefully folding one into the other. Like flour and sugar, eggs and butter. Folding ingredients, adding an air cushion. Mixing worldly remains with soul and memory. The fine bone particles tinkling over each other. A fine dust rising out the of the bucket coating the nearby surfaces in the kitchen. The dust rises up in a lazy heavy way. Suspended for moments before blooming and falling content. I have the desire, as I have since their deaths, to put something in my mouth. Something their hands have touched. Licking surfaces. Mouthing surfaces. Or choking down these ashes. But I am a coward.

This mixing is not a rush job. With every pour and mix I must wait minutes until they settle down. Agitated as they are to be together. Her darker fold over his lighter, embracing familiarity. In his I find a little piece of metal, wonder if it came from him or the apparatus of cremation. Him, a little stick of metal, interior surgery, war shrapnel. Rubbing bone on bone, smudging dust together on their way to the final journey. Death is not the final journey. Funeral is not the final journey. Even cremation is not the final journey. For my parents. Deaths that have taken over seventy years to achieve. Ashes that have waited seven months to mingle. Final journeys take longer than life sometimes. This is their beginning.

Ashes are Bone and Dust

When the bone fragments arc to earth
the wind picks up the dust from the ashes
before they settle to the ground
separating them on the wing
and blows the dust out off the summit of the hill
across the countryside
          it is then the magic happens
as the wind has along its body
particles of the dust
a cloud that forms and reforms
moving out over the land in a mobile body
as if the two spirits are truly joining
contemplating each other for a moment
rolling and swirling and forming
in a comfortable courtship of familiarity
moving more slowly than the wind
a heavy mass suspended but travelling out
over the leaden quality of the stillness of Wiltshire
I fully expect their two figures to become visible
and smile down on me before melting
on the cradle of the wind.

Horningsham

It is flatter than I remember
flaxen green image of farmland
and quiet   as if everyone is working outside the village
at the big house   or in the fields
stone walls, quiet vegetable gardens beyond
cemetery grown high with grasses straining to meet
the bend of an oak tree
my grandmother is buried here
the plot undiscovered
thumbing through parish records   she appears
on parchment-thick paper   ink that blackens green
quill stroke of history   my history
we were Jews once removed then   twice more
and our signatures were X's
labouring on the land and in the woods

The village has the stalled feeling of a walled city
standing stones   deserted feel of no young people
community of like-named   three family trees
run through its citizens   my cousin, my cousin
my father lived in this house   or this one
I have a choice   blended by old photographs
two boys, two girls and a mother scowling
under a thatched roof
a road in and a road out

In a cottage past the Bath Arms
chocolate-box rat's-nest home
a woman who remembers my father as a boy
rode the bus to Frome with my aunt

In the perfectly tended eccentric garden
house number 102 spelled out in topiary
a man talks about my uncle
the name Battson he remembers

A woman gives me tea   she is related to us
fits a piece in the puzzle of names
fetches sepia school photographs   my father and his siblings
he is cross-legged on the floor with a crooked tie
she is mischievous in her smile, the dark curl, cunning eye
he stands grown up at the back, serious
the other one is missing
here are the absent young of the village
one-roomed schoolhouse
stone building and cobblestones nicked by a thousand knees

It is emptier than I remember
The post office closed for a long lunch
newsagent's door squeaks open on loose hinges
a puff of torpid air
small selection of sweets   yesterday's newspapers
a slow buzzing fly   drunk and lingering
quiet   as if everyone still works at the big house
my grandmother is buried in this plot   or this one
there is no headstone to mark the grave
no photograph for me to know
        no parents to point the way.

The Dead in My Dreams

Hiss and a diluted smell of natural gas as the radiator bleeds air, shoots out blue-black liquid in a spray against the tangerine wall. I've been dreaming about death again. The characters in my dreams not realizing that they're dead, or perhaps they are in denial. So they languish in spaces until I, the dreamer, possessor of the dream, inform them that they are dead. The radiator, relieved of the gaseous burden pumps red hot into the chilled room. Now I can open the windows to let out the stale smell of smoke and cabbage leaching through from the neighbour's apartment. In the dream the dead ones often stand around lighting cigarettes and not being aware of one another in the room, until suddenly they notice a shadow or a small movement, then they are able to join the others. The silver birch outside my room has lost all its leaves now, they coat the ground a bright yellow. The maple tree still full of waving orange leaves like waxy gold sunlight, shadow and light. Sometimes when I point out to the dead that they are, in fact, dead, they'll go through mock hysterics and act out a kind of theatrical death throe, often more gruesome than real death. The scene will choke me until I wake, the pillow wet, my chest full of emptiness and my body a weary weight on the bed, strangely relaxed and calm. After several weeks of warm fall weather the winter is breaking over the city. Today I walked in the ravine, shuffling through dry leaves and their almost mouldy autumn smell. My raincoat was open and flop flapping around my legs, anchored by my hands in pockets, the wind burning across my cheeks. In the valley below the streets most of the trees have shed their leaves, gone are the multitude of red oak, orange maple, yellow birch, all crisply reduced to brown and grey before mulching into mud and early leaf skeletons. It's most upsetting when the dead board subway trains which I cannot enter. I stand distraught on the platform while they glow eerily off to unknown destinations, wearing baseball caps backward with logos of their favourite teams pulsing out. In my neighbourhood piles of the gold brown leaves rustle from sidewalk to gutter. When the sun sets, long leaf shadows play on concrete, and lawns stretch to houses where windows spill primrose light, a welcome to the dead and the living.

Voices from Beyond I

The smooth saturated night
drifts the songs of crickets
through my bedroom window
I am thinking about the ceiling fan
thwocking   slowly   around
moments before sleep obliterates tension
I roll comfortably toward the window
then
my father's voice clear in my ear
as he speaks my name.

Voices from Beyond II

Northbound train clanking and howling
past me on the subway platform
at Davisville
its undertow suck rattling
my morning newspaper
I can hear the tinny swosh beat
from a boy's headphones
then
from somewhere near the waiting room
my father calls my name.

What happened after the photograph was taken

In the photograph my father is in love with me
the bridge of his large nose rubs
the smooth skin of my baby forehead
his eyes fixed on my mine
a crinkling of humour hatches there
the moment before a full smile
he is wearing a thinly striped shirt
underneath a ribbed sweater
    —I remember the smell of his sweaters, wood, wool, fath

In the photograph I have the same ear shape as him
but it'll be years before I grow into the chin, the jaw
the way his long face flattens across the cheekbone
his foreshortened top lip and large bottom lip
    —kissable, like a saxophonist's, my mother said
I love that face in a narcissistic reflection
it's the late '50s, his hair is short, sideburns long
my baby fluff showing red even
in the black and white photograph
    —he carried a lock of it in his wallet until
I was in my twenties

The photograph ends below our chins, my mother,
instead of hacking off heads
framed low so there is much space above us
makes the picture surreal and crooked
an isolated feel of summer in England
him and me in the world
in the photograph waves break on an almost deserted beach
a spit or pier lolls out into the sea on the horizon

a lady behind a windbreak attempts a tan
a tap bound to a wooden post grows out
of my father's left shoulder

The photograph sits on my desk and reminds me of loss
nobody can tell me where it was taken
what time of day or year
who was there, what they spoke of
I expect my sister was in the background
with her thirteen-year-old pout
there was probably a striped windbreak
some wooden deckchairs
a Primus stove brewing up tea, a child's spade and bucket
my father probably held me in his lap
I expect he stroked my cheek
encouraged me to grasp his finger in my fist
wondered at this tiny miracle in his non-verbal way

what happened after the photograph was taken was this:
thirty-seven years later he was dead.

Evening in Paris

There was always a midnight blue glass bottle
on my mother's dressing table
fluted and spiralled, an oval silver stamp on the front
twisted Arabian lid
keeping a harem of French perfume under its rubber seal
Evening in Paris
my sister told me our mother soaked pieces of cotton wool in
pushed it between breast and bra
I just remember the bottle on the dressing table
the smell of that perfume
heady, round and custardy, the fragrance of gardenia
stayed with me always
choice of flowers that stops me dead, inhaling deep breaths
straining my lungs to get more,
              the white flower ground to memories

It must have been the late '60s when they discontinued it
my mother's stash evaporating over time
little blue bottles secreted around the house
in bedside tables, the writing desk, between underwear
and mother's request was always
"if you see any Evening in Paris at the airport..."
"...in Harrods", "...on the boat"
until it was clear that women who wore blood-red lipstick
and Evening in Paris were an endangered species

When we went through her things after she died
I was surprised that those little blue bottles of comfort
didn't show up
my childhood memories were strung with them

forming a border around the pictures of home, of mother
like fairy lights around a balcony

Then we heard that Evening in Paris was being brought back
my sister took up the cause, searching everywhere
saleswomen at department stores told us, "it's coming soon"
but we haven't found it
and every time I'm with her, my sister says
"if you see any Evening in Paris at the duty free..."
"...in Harrods", ..."at Selfridges"
and I remember my mother all over again.

Carpenter

He is in the rush, rush clang of the small factory
wood and sawdust, high frequency whiz buzz
of the circular saw
its excited pitch as it chews through planks,
sheets, cords, unfortunate fingers
smell of machine oil underneath exuberant sap
aroma of new cut wood
pile of utilitarian school furniture spills out with sawdust
into the rain-wet forecourt, damp asphalt,
cigarette smoke and tannic tea
every man takes a job to support his passion
women; football; beer; the whirls of grain in blond oak
amber speckles of polished bird's-eye maple
a handcrafted writing desk, sensual as a woman's curves
this piece of furniture

he is a carpenter and he is a Carpenter
and he is my father

Three generations back a man stands
dappled under oak leaf sunlight
in a Wiltshire forest
caught bright blade axe head, worn wooden handle
salty tang of sweat across shoulders under musky hessian
green wood smell pinches nostrils
every man takes a job to support his family
his calloused, work-stiff hands close
over his wife's on the kitchen table
in lamplight, a glass of flat, redolent amber ale reflects softly
on the beeswax-smooth oak surface

wood cut over many months, dovetail joints, wooden pegs
labour of love, of necessity
this piece of furniture

he is a Carpenter and he is a carpenter and he is a woodsman
and he is my father's great-grandfather.

Four Years of Census

found piece

In a house called The Butts
1797
Ben Carpenter, alias Tinse, shoemaker
Children: 1 male and 1 female under 7
3 males and 1 female above 7
House is old but tolerable

In a house on Church Street
1799
Ben Carpenter, alias Tense, shoemaker
Children: 1 male and 2 females under 7
3 males and 1 female above 7
House is in good repair, man industrious,
wife has bad health, obliged to seek relief from parish

The street, house of John Moody
1801
Ben Carpenter, alias Trice,
Children: 2 males and 1 female under 7
3 males and 1 female above 7.

Full Moon Family History

When I walk down from the hillside the moon is full
our imaginations, our illicit dreams
mapped out against our desires
a streak of airplane flotsam blossoming out
beside the puzzled face of the planet
and although somewhere, tonight, the moon will shine full
here at 10 in the morning it is 500 mile blue sky
and the promise of spring
I think nothing about the moon, my feelings
the primitive swell in my body

There is a story that my great-grandfather,
a travelling salesman, one day never returned home
left his wife, their two sons, never to be seen again
dead or another family somewhere
no one ever really knew for certain
one son, great-uncle Albert, died during the war
when his hot-air balloon was shot down
there is a story that his brother, my grandfather
a thin, unremarkable man, close-eyed and wax-moustached
was a bastard, not in familial terms
but because he pleased himself
from what I hear lately, his own children hated him
all except Esme, apple of her father's eye
who came home pregnant from a one-night stand
when she was already married to a soldier serving overseas
there is a story that my paternal grandfather
married my grandmother under a shotgun
both of them lying about their ages
in a time when men should always be older than their women

Sid was born four months later
          there is a story that my grandmother's sister
gave birth to a bastard child
she was brought up by my great-grandmother as one of her ow
Doris played the piano with the long fingers of the innocent

I am immersed in the pepper custard smell of wisteria
hanging mauve like a deflated bunch of grapes
wafting out on the May-warmed evening
sun dispelling spring iciness of air
hint of mown grass, the bleating of lambs
moon silvering the night sky
blotting out the galaxies with its bold light
a light for lovers, for travellers
but now we barely leave our homes for it
in my pyjamas, a desire strong as passion
to be out under moon
feel the omniscient blue-light beacon stretching over me
wet grass surprise
a midnight dew on my feet, there is a slug adopting sandals

          There is a story that I was descended from
novelists and gentry
looking up into the branches of the tree
I see labourers and illiterates who sign their names "X"
or get someone else to
and a plethora of illegitimates
ranging hidden behind my middle-class image
sharing the same cold moon
the same warm blood of arrangement.

Laid out at St. Mark's

Just before midnight on a sleeting
November New York street
I walk out of the weather
into St. Mark's bookstore, rush of dry heat
contrasting the cold of my clothes against tired skin
soporific warmth, the smell of paper, dust of books
in my cold-sharpened nostrils
milling around the new release table
my fingers run over book jackets, flip through pages
until I come to a book
the photographic story of a policeman
at the front of the 1900s
a book of the dead
suicides in baths, men with their brains
blown out on kitchen tiles
women with gaping holes in naked raped abdomens
smothered children, a look of trusting surprise remaining
the pornography of murder
I cannot tear my eyes from the pages
photograph after photograph my mind chokes
here is a boy laid out, here a woman
here two Hispanic men, oily hair dishevelled, laid out
my brain sees the image of my mother in her coffin
in commonality are the necks
in every image of cadavers laid out
the neck pushes into the shoulders
blossoming with creases
from collarbone to chin
there is a heat rushing up my body
then a coldness from the forehead down

when it reaches my throat I feel nauseated
my eyes lose focus, the cotton-wool head of fainting
I close the book quickly
place it gently back on the table for fear
of waking the inhabitants,
and flee the shop, stumbling over a stroller
dropping my scarf
knocking into customers in my hurry to get outside
chill dark air, my shirt damp with panic
and away from the nausea of memories.

Holiday

for Kim

The unconscious sends up warning flares into the conscious
seductive smokey gunpowder
masking the pinprick light festival
taking the edge off the pain

Small steps, a unlucid day trip
before diving into the surrender
fumbled oblivion of nautical abstraction
it is the wind blowing hot summer air through
overburdened fruit trees
leaf rustle — uni-directional noise-swirl
a constant through every open window in your mind
whipping up fallen blossoms over footsteps
and confusing the logical order of numbers
a heat on your tiredness!
the woozy feeling of deprivation
and the comfort! the comfort!
of not needing to know when.

Orange

And then this, the teasing of hair
from the cloistered darkness of brooding vegetables
to a peaking sunspot
gold waving over the sphere
under the influence of autumn leaves and ambient music
Moroccan slippers and the slip to a covered chaise
rolled blankets and pillows, a corner of thought
it's the paint that tells us what we are
what we should put down for posterity
pumpkin wind blowing coldly
cracks in the windows, the chill of empty living
and me missing keys, living in the shadow of MS
shift of colour
pigment falling dark to the drain
a bleached remainder of reality
what we were like before artifice
sunbird, sunflower
the retina-open brightness I want to be.

On Seeing Safia

When I speak she recognizes my voice
calculating memories in sapphire clearness
empty abacus screen, the beads waiting for patterns
where ideas are stored and history formed
past lives and alien interpretations
through mere centimetres she heard me speak
floated silent as I whispered through sleep
a seashell's shush and the beating of two hearts
felt my palm, the warm substance of healing
and heard me speak, the hum dull and sometimes ragged
from rooms and corners of rooms
the flat softness of mattress
through the variant ambience of street
car interiors and greyhound bus stations
words from a poem filtered through auras
over clinking silverware in crowded Indian restaurants
sound floating on amniotic fluid, a vast ocean of language
languid
and she heard my voice through telephone cables
over thousands of kilometres on different continents
she heard it accompanied by the somnolent hiss of rain
before she had ears she reverberated with my timbre
before conception
now she hears me speak clear and without mediation
looks my way, the slow turn of recognition
and it is there
in the deep-written pockets of a tabula rasa memory
when I speak she recognizes my voice.

Desperation

I am driving through the streets of Delhi
in a heated stunned sickness
I am walking beside canals in Venice
holding the hand of a man I don't know
when you fall asleep in the open air
it feels like madness
I am climbing the hill at Sigiriya
to the point of salvation
I am kissing my sister's lips
on a hillside in Wiltshire
when you listen to the voice in the wind
it feels like there is no tomorrow
I am lurking in back streets of Barcelona
hanging with the whores
I am heartbeaten at the castle of Visegrád
seduced by a another woman's husband
when you cut yourself preparing food
it feels like you are almost there
I am trancing in the palace at Samode
mistaking Seconal for Tylenol
I am sweating on the pavement in Austin
sleeping in a stranger's bed
when you travel rapid continents
it feels like desperation
I am marble-blind at the Taj Mahal
looking for redemption
I am sitting at my desk in Toronto
trying to figure out what hit me.

Creation

Pau pupping bag hits surface, blue dust wafts soulful
ice-blue laundry trick for whiter-than-whites in summer sparkle
tracing non-repro blue
bristles spread out when paint load is depressed
curve steady with hand dexterity
sweeping lick brush traces letters
the humours sweeping onto white corrugated board
yellow, green, red, black
three fonts spread words over oval
overlapping ascenders and descenders
the f tail trailing into t's stalk
phrase's repetitive journey into eye and brain.

Bronzing with Michael

for AMA

It's a gold crazy kind of love we have
standing beside you this frigid January afternoon
hands stuffed in the pockets of our tweed coats
looking like Paris 1934, the buried retro-ness of you
in the misty winter afternoon twilight of the barn interior
sharp smell of fire, the heated kiss, water on hot metal hiss
there is a lightness inside me when I think of you
like long-parted lovers
we hold each other by the arm
walking like conspirators against the ordinary

Three men tamping down sand in oil drums
containment for molten metal
arms semaphore arc as biceps ripple down
thin metal pole in each hand
breath frozen on the air, shifting crystalline cloud
raw the way manual labour is
I follow your gaze along the lines of their bodies
resting on noses that are large and defined
European ancestry shows in each face

Six short plaster columns enclose a bounty
baked for days
standing stones in a brick kiln enclosure
awaiting their centuries
the sculpted wax has melted within the cast
a rose impression, the leaves and thorns
while the moon rises and falls, three times

There is suspension in the air
a shallow breath excitement
we huddle in our coats, brush away the white plaster dust
silicone that stands on the point of each wool thread
a dewdrop for the invisible
packed blue snow nuggets outside the open barn door
the crucible of molten bronze burning green in the pit

Six drums and their precious inhabitants
wait cradled in the mounds of sand
the crucible inching its way on ceiling-high metal runners
through soft, chilled air
pours into each plaster cast a ribboned shot of boiling metal
orange liquid sun plummets down and then bubbling
shoots out in a tangerine globule
and introverts
slowly blackens like cooling amber
viscous, then opaque
it is a compelling desire to place one's finger in the shiny sun
into your soul
the torture of cauterizing a tongue with hot metal

And then the artist
his pickaxe thudding into the supine column
rakes over the plaster, still radiating heat
to pick out the chicken-wire frame
inside, the bronze born, still singing, still malleable, and black
folds itself out, clinging to its conception of wax
each rose stem hosed down in the snow
hissing of water, steam dragging ragged into the air
the evolution of sculpture

We take our leave of the bronzing barn
light fingertips as you brush the thin white powder from me
my cheek, my hair
this gold crazy love spinning out from us
reddening winter sky, smell of metal and heated bodies
this laughing inside to hysteria
calmness of blood surging through bodies
we kiss each other on the cheeks like Parisians
and drive away for another month.

Humpty Dumpty in the Pink City

Jaipur 1998

We are watching Jaipur from a flat roof
on the highest building in the circle
10 rupees a visitor to the toothless creature
with black fingernails
in India everything has a price
the sienna-stained street is a marketplace
of heaped red carrots
orange chiffon saris swollen by the breeze
piebald goats and dusty chestnut cows
chew cud around a fountain in the centre of the circle
their owners leaving them all day to be fed
by pious Hindus, vegetables scattered around bored animals
cycle rickshaws whip danger and tourists along the road
dirt and exhaust fumes, layer of dust from sandal to knee
brushed pale over many brown legs
pink facade of the palace of the winds
washed umber by a setting sun

The crumbling wall we lean over
leaves pink dust on our clothes
below us the pink city is a jumbled mass of vehicles
and ox carts
waves of colourful clothes and trodden flower heads
through this chaos, an uneven procession of weaving,
leaping men in white
several break away, run up and down the column
shouting and throwing flowers
our western shock sees they are carrying
a cardboard coffin on their shoulders

open to the skies, to us
its cargo lolls from side to side in his robes
blooms garlanded around his neck reflect clouds
a sight so commonplace we are the only ones staring
and from this height we can see the man was older
closed sunken eyes in dark face, grey streaked beard
his head covered white
we, recently bereaved, are transfixed

Indian funeral processions end with a burning pyre
open dry sticks igniting
coffin smoldering, the body leaking its oil
crowing, the ravens wait in nearby treetops
the final act in Hindu funeral ritual is when the oldest son
steps forward to break open the top of his father's skull
a gnarled hardwood club
constriction of biceps as it hits home
bone splitting apart to release the father's spirit.

Barcelona Whores

And coming up from the Palace Guell
I turn into a side street leading to the market, dark and dank
straight out of a Jean Genet story
with its attendant striped-shirt '30s bar culture
and the sun catches itself
folding away to a larger street with flowers and opportunities
this quiet street harbours sadness
as if everyone's breath is caught up in a moment of
anticipation
regret
the cobbles echoing medieval footfalls
paranoia of syphilitic sailors
distant bright sky tubing down through buildings
top-lighting the damp pavement
reflecting a white wash up into
the shadow cavern faces of men
burly from bullrings and fishing boats
the only women on the street are the whores
on the afternoon shift
clicking their tongues at the men
turning on ample hips and angling their faces
tangle of black curls caught up with fishbone combs
they are old, these whores, and their multitudinousness
surprises me out of my tourist torpor
they are red-lipped and grey-skinned
black-stockinged legs, their red-feathered bodices
flash seductively in the polished gloom of moist walls
here she kisses her head close to a younger whore
here she waves up at a woman leaning
clutching a baby toward laundry strung over the street

and here she measures the length of me
        it's a possibility
three-minute walk through the Genet story
then I cross a passage, the border
where the sun catches up and joins me
smell of strawberries and chocolate
women pushing children in prams, dragging bags of vegetabl
chatter, catcalling,
whisper of bicycles passing on the drying cobbles
white sangria afternoon
and I don't look back
in case I break the spell.

Santa Maria del la Pieta

for Armando '98 and my sister '99

In this church, the yellow sandstone of Venice
I am shivering myself into my jacket
against the evening cold salt damp
of the recently walked quay
where flagstones reflect the blue-tinged orange
of fierce gaslights
pits and dips smoothed by a million rains
the high raking of lagoon waters
and the toned leather of Venetian gentry
flagstones rush toward the church

Plush burgundy velvet curtains
soothe floor as they part to let me inside
I am standing looking up into a vaulted oval room
mostly altar
Tiepolo's coronation of the Virgin Mary
sweeping up above the candy-red glass lamps
church and concert hall for the adjoining hospital
the patients becoming famous throughout Europe
for their musical skills
and Antonio Vivaldi as their master, the church composer

Sitting on the ungiving wooden pews for hours
in Vivaldi's church
my joints stiffen and ache in the damp chill
I am transfixed by the chamber orchestra
all strings and black clothes
as they play the Red Priest's music on the floor
where it was composed

subtlety of notes blossom out
as he would have heard it
writing for these stone walls, this vaulted chapel, for god
twinged rough whine of resin on catgut
illuminated notes to the heavens, to spring and autumn

And played here too, an Albinoni passage
I hear my mother's funeral in this music
the long notes for our extended slow walk behind the coffin
in the chapel overlooking a spring Hertfordshire countryside
here I sit among strangers, tears flooding my eyes
dragging grey streaks of mascara down my cold cheeks
stones with a heartbeat of music
softly give into this concert
it's like living, a robust wine-bloom of sound
the chapel smiling to hear
Vivaldi's masterpieces resonate again.

Figuring it Out

It took days of solitude
brisk walks over century canals
eating pasta coloured with squid ink
a glass to my lips, the sharp fruitiness of wine
to realize the metaphors were gone
emotion had faded
that my life, transitional, stretched over me
like tissue skin under an autopsy knife
and peeling back slowly
because we are all stretched taut
waiting for a split to flay us
when at last I resigned myself
it is too long, but nothing can be done to hurry it
and there is this waiting to deal with.

In June Country

for Kurt's stepfather

Countryside spreads out before me, corn high
never-ending newness of washed saturation
long light, the crystal sharpness of leaves, green
standing still while life rushes by
a long sigh, a jazz tune, the peppery sounds of America
       Jumpin' Jimenez   we say in Latin American
I feel like static, the grey dust of a million stones at my feet
place myself on a hard shoulder, sun beating down
buzz of flies, a growl of motorcycles, trucks
highway to nowhere quickly by foot
it is a hard slog, a sweat-covered walk

Off the intersection are fields, fields
crickets and sun, full mailboxes, flags up
hum of a tractor churning at soil
between rows of soybean plants
birds scatter above broken earth
under the cool and pleasant trees planted here
by footfall, the fabric of jeans
my shoulders are raw, radiating from the sun

Blue whitewashed farm holds remnants
from more than a full life
a sow oiler forgotten under brambles
black raspberry shriveled by the season
a century barn, strewn with the debris of six-score history
cadillac, dodge truck, oil cans and glass jugs
two buggies, leather raccoon-eaten, perch in the rafters
we hold hands to history, the poignant growth of cancer

and time does stand still
is this love? The dog at my legs says yes
the look in your eyes says yes
the splendid RV says yes

Waving away from the black walnut, the broken windmill
we pace gravel dust, again and again
tall grasses by the creek sway under interference
sun moves relentlessly toward night
lady-killer full moon of card games and chance
revolving toward midnight
the dark countryside breathes out its cool rustle of cornstalks.

Grey Dog on Red Scrub

Winter in the Rio Grande Canyon, New Mexico

At midnight I wake with a desert/wine dry mouth
in the burnt-wood scented bedroom
a line in my head is there for the taking
like a long-forgotten dream
out of comfort the wide pine boards soothe my soles
a slip of sand-coloured paper
on the cobalt-tiled vanity in the bathroom I write:
     Grey Dog on Red Scrub
and the poem begins.

There are two sets of boot prints
and a dog's paw in light snow
covering only the well-trodden sand
airplanes too high to hear
a white comet tail in the cyan sky
omen of the millennium
in the desert canyon sounds are suspended
lonely pip-pip call of a fluttering bird
answered in kind and gunshot over the mountain
three deer freeze behind brush
their white-rimmed ears full attention
on the grey dog on red scrub
scenting their air but not seeing
green-tipped sage bushes
dissolve dry in aroma released rubbed fingertips
red volcanic-pocked rock with two green stones for eyes
man-made lizard built from the canyon's life
the grey dog runs on Georgia O'Keeffe country

watches the dust rise on the gravel switchback
a solitary vehicle threads silently up to meet the sky

Later when I return chilled to the bed
I dream I am looking out across the Taos road
down over the gorge we walked that noon
and beyond, the forest plain, with a truck raising dust,
stretches away to Abiquiu
and a red-dirt house rising on a mesa
hearing your soft sleep breath on the pillow.

Crosses on the Median

This is where you left the highway, Cheryl Hicks
the car rolling over and over
into the concave median, sod and glass spurting
you are dead by the time the state trooper gets to you

The curve is too sharp for your speed, Bobby Menendez
truck raking through the iron barrier, ripped rubber
hillside's impact concertinaing the engine into your seat
you are dead when running fieldworkers
bring crowbars to pry you out

What happened to your car, Hank Lee?
the road is straight here, double-sided smooth asphalt
no dips, no curves, no barriers, no hillsides, no ice
but four of you perished here
in the America of roadside crosses

Palomino shakes its head in slow motion
hawk hovers above grass
dead coyote leaves pieces of itself for a hundred yards
along the highway
blood lumps and fur impossible to imagine how
and the interstates thread patchwork states together
a seamless journey through catastrophes and beauty
metal and flesh fusion that works like oil and water

Cheryl Hicks's white cross on the median
is hung with purple orchids, her name calligraphied onto the wc
a small teddy bear is tied to the base
arms open to passing drivers

Bobby Menendez's cross hammered into the rock hillside
bends toward the road with the weight of
christmas wreath about its white shoulders
fully decorated christmas tree sparkles below
in the setting sun

Someone has mowed the grass leading to Hank Lee's cross
his three friends stand beside him like a roadside Gomorrah
flowers bloom in the remembering earth at their feet

This is the America of painted deserts
arable plains, mountains
and roadside crosses
each a testament that marks the shoulders of roads
like a southern belle's beauty spot
white cross shrines to the interstates' sacrificial appetite
luminous wood humming through fog, rain and darkness
decorated by survivors who warn the sightless drivers
of the power of destiny.

White Dwarf on Curdled Sky

The full moon is in earth's shadow
       second contact
umbra the colour of curdled blood
a shadow that tells the woes of the planet
and somewhere behind us
the sun burns retinas in a southern hemisphere
practicing for red gianthood
       its surface to cool and expand
       burning away from scarlet nebula, ghost of energy
       the star's core shrinking to white density
       mass of the sun compressed into the size of the earth
       matter is a ton a teaspoon
           in the lonely theatre of space
           performances unfold in light-years of darkness
           seemingly unchanged
       white dwarfs: Sirius, Cassiopeia
       flirting with heavenly companions
and swirling over my head
earth's clouded crimson shadow
a moment filled with silent animals
an uneasy darkness
white frost breath suspended

first eclipse of the millennium.

Diving off the Bridge

for H.S.

When I heard you jumped off the Bloor Street viaduct
early Thursday morning, a goodbye note in your pocket
I gulped air in disbelief, wondering what made you so drastic
knowing, in my heart, exactly what did
I saw you two weeks ago in Starbucks
feeling ill — I think of you now every time I drive over the bridge
or travel through it in a subway car
suspended over the abyss
staring north over the river, the Don Valley Parkway, the woods
blossoming out in new, bright early summer light
look away before it all gets too gruesome
before I'm drawn to the edge
and it unnerves me, the parallels between our lives
histories and definitions of failure
that image bigger than the reality
the frightening thing is that I didn't think of you as a loser
I feel wobbly at the instantaneousness of your choice
my mind loose and swinging
reeling with a horror of the inevitable
the difficulty of creating in this world, in our heads
destiny seems shaped by constant striving for the elusive
disregarding our own successes as small
even the Nobel Prize, once attained,
       would be reduced to nothing for us
your ironic theatricality that made me smile
last-minute phone calls to friends in the early hours of morning
       imagine waking up to that horror
letters to people posted the night before
a pile of instructions for after the death, an erased hard drive

help me, help me
I would have done those things too
I've practiced for it every day
and I find myself wondering what clothes you chose to wear
you don't always die, you know, when you jump
you don't always succeed
did you think of that?

Equivalence/Love

I saw a photograph of John Steinbeck on the back of one of his books in a store on Queen Street and thought how much he looked liked the men in my family. Or perhaps the men in my family all have that look from the '30s— gaunt, short-haired and slightly melancholy.

The second time I met you I had the same feeling. Perhaps it was the haircut, or your shirt sleeves rolled up high on your bicep like an English queer-boy. But I kept looking at your face, thinking how much you looked like my father — younger than I remember him, of course. And you felt it too, not that I looked like your father, or your mother for that matter, but a recognition, the feeling that you're seeing someone for the first time, really looking at them.

That moment lasted for minutes, us just smiling and looking around each other's face. A visual exploration where we heard nothing of what the other said. And for a few days afterwards I was in love with you. The reflection of family, the familiarity of looks, the narcissism of self. Just like when I was in love with John Steinbeck for that few hours after I left the bookstore and wandered along Queen Street thinking about family, the possibilities of love.

Futility of Desire

How many times must I check my voice mail
before I realize you're not going to call
spend hours working over the "what if" scenarios
in them becoming strong, tender, rude, forgiving
as the stomach flutters into ribs
the wanting swells my tongue
a "call you tomorrow" promise
stretches over 3 days, 5 days
   I am not part of your Banana Republic scene
   I am not one of the pseudo arts crowd
   I am feeling very sorry for myself
but the calm part of me wonders what happened
how you forgot about me so completely
our epic conversations meant nothing
don't want to think of you as manipulative, insensitive, fickle
or guarded against me
I am not ready for the game of who gives in first
forfeit and weakness, the power dynamic of desire
but my body still remembers your touch
misses the warm fragrance of your skin
small considerations you showed
in sweetness of tender actions
and why does this teenaged angst
not stay with its own age group
with you, I was ready to write informed by desire
instead an ugly rejection steps in
I am not prepared for another round of loss.

A Goodbye Poem

for Laurent

And in this moment I realize I cannot write a thing about love. The wind blowing through the window on goose-bumped skin, the way night turns into day for the sleep deprived, the way my heart aches for you. Everything I believed, or thought I believed is empty, like a blackened highway in a David Lynch film. A simple gesture, a realization that what I expected to be reciprocated, wasn't even thought of, except with annoyance. An intrusion on the excitement of life, the plasticity of existence and what we believe to be real for us. A train breezing midnight in the distance, the breath that takes us from town to town, its course denying the real. Moments between families, discussions between lovers, the unwanted message that truth brings. It is constant like flax, like disappointment, like the course of my tears. Then, echoing in the distance, the truth smacks you like a romance novel. Time spent wasting with smiles and nonsense, the euphoric feeling that this is love and the broad smile that comes by just walking, just noticing the world. The slap that contorts, built on a kiss, a chance encounter. Something that changes when intimacy is involved, the shift that makes it more real, more tangible and more dangerous. Gentle gestures, a honeyed stickiness on salt landscape would never end except by proxy. And there is nothing else really, a touch, a kiss, the building of lop-sided dreams. The truth heard in bright car interiors with the engine running, a feeling of nihilism. It is this that changes me from the imagined importance. Colour of rubbed oak in sunlight, the texture of your skin, finding your small hairs in the sink. The infatuation that means everything in the essence of the world: the small breath, the colour of water, the smell of rain. And when I stay up past 1 a.m. listening to small movements of raccoons, the breath on a cotton landscape. Moon that rises and wanes in terrible light, a chance pulling of tides, a body of salt. It troubles me, like iodine, like the wrinkled necks of the dead, like insouciance or disinterest and I question my existence. The small smattering of fancy or the spark of life. Is it all worth it? Which memories will we take with us? The swimming lyricism of paintings, a last breath of a stanza, the mute kiss of a lover? And there is nothing compared to this: lying awake under the truth of you, the wide-eyed sleeplessness of lost dreams.

Missing

driving across a hot and startling America
there is nothing about Toronto I will miss

except you, I practice lines of postcards I will write
exotic places, exciting news you will probably dismiss

instead the desert warms my bones, my soul, contrasts
drenching humidity of eastern summer no one can miss

under a windblown sky and the promise of rain
I size up umbrellas accompanied by "can I help you miss"

I lie between soft comfort, after dreaming about you
noting the fading intensity with which I miss

you, fading like eventual chili stains on white
the yearning I felt, I can almost begin to dismiss

as the packed days heal along, I have to ask
was it you, or the thought of you that I really miss.

Antithesis

The desert is not New York City
the Chrysler Building does not torpedo its spires
into this indigo/red sky
or upside down into the scrub-covered earth
like an alien's rack of finger stalls
there is not the yellow pallor of a living smog
or the shake of underground trains with their sharp piss smell

Men with crack-slurred speech
ingrained with dirt from the street
do not jangle their KFC cups at you
there are not knuckle-driven pallets
transporting vets with no legs
along the crests of mountain rims
nor is there the excitement
of walking along Avenue B
dodging milk-stained night children
and Nuyorican poets.

**When I invited the rest of the class on a morning hike
I was met by silence**

If when the others in my workshop are sleeping
rolling over in high-altitude dry-mouthed sleep
or eating a pre-proscribed breakfast
and the day is chill with dry-crackle sage brush
against the stony desert

If I in my unsuitable white sneakers
plod upward desperately, sweatily
peeling my morning orange
and pocketing the peel
saying to myself
       I am fit
       I am healthy
       I am sanctimonious

If I take stock of my aching buttocks
my overheated feet
my city-pale legs against the lichen-covered rock
who shall say I am not
the happy masochist of my class?

Aspects of Breast

at the ash-swirled alter, tubercular English writer
stirring tremulous movement in my homesick breast

in the coffin her skin cold and musky
fingers laced with cotton handkerchief across breast

the sky skims orange/umbra threads indigo
silhouetting silent-standing pines along the mountain's breast

afternoon drops heat through muslin
your cool hard hand cradles the flesh of my breast.

Rain Series

on tongue hint of heat
metal dampness of sky taste
green chili smoothness

> the damp of soft pine smell
> tang of grey danger
> primal warning to shelter

claming over skin
the wind's breath cool and close
sky reaches to earth

> wind rustles, rumbles
> cracking over mountains
> weather-pattern war

heavy grey clouds drop
flume mystic rain-bed curtains
over blue mountains

Italianos Canyon

for Ben

And I
walking through shadow-deepened forest toward a half moon
saying my poem prayers into the evening
for love, for remembrance, for you
pines blazing green through a sunset of flame
their long shadows peaking over mountain ridge
across small glittering waterfalls
that blend rocks, pebbles and bank
it is your touch that brings me through heaven
sifted eyes the colour of clouded midnight
you are touch when gentle touch is all
a firm hand cupping the desperate flesh of my buttock
gleaming night sweat on your shoulders
shifting blue in the dragon-light of a melting candle
our shoulders rest on soft beds
a reminder of wood on hip bones
a place tender on breast bone, the inside of knees
and I
walking through evening-deepened forest
toward a full moon
the cicadas click when stars puncture sky
over the soft rustle of rushing animals
will miss you, remembering the musk-sage smell of your skin
a silent kiss over the enormity of the sky.

Lulling Language

The wide window sills are filled with soft
water-smoothed river stones
I think of you with each one I caress
speaking French in a room of strangers, Americans
we eat fresh, falcon-killed duck, full rich tang on the tongue
wash of tannic red wine over blue teeth
the Paris I remember
is roasted coffee-scented streets, their pavements
wet with overflowing buckets jammed with fresh flowers
and you, the smell of apricots
your café au lait skin in the setting light
you twist your face up toward tourist attics and gargoyles
your comfortable elegant long-legged gait
walking the mile that is Paris

And we talk Parisian French in an adobe kitchen
in the middle of snow-laden sagebrush desert
switch between several languages in our pretension
but the sound of Europe soothes me, a memory, a history
the lulling of sweetness, comfortable switch
from alien articulation of American
even this southwestern softness
river stone in my palm, a pebble laid on the back of my tongue
the American-French you speak
float me on that language.

Sage Series

dry sage, slightly acrid
lies on the tongue like lamb's ears
to melt like soft metal

       bundles bound by string
       wrapped like a rush-bound baby
       leaves crushed against stalks

burn sweet sage, dispel
sewer spirits of my room
warm desert in sun

       a dry prickle, soft
       yet pliant, echo of life
       blackened oiliness

it crackles when lit
blue/red flame hissing out breath
and sighs its smoke out

Alone at Stephen's

The stillness magnifies itself in the clear air of the mountains
a hawk circles, riding thermals, sharp wing feathers
flaked slate against sky
piñon rustles almost imperceptibly
aura of warmed resin at the back of nose
as wine infuses my blood
grey-blanket heat around shoulders
in the crisp winter sunlight on blue chairs
overlooking the rugged gorge
dropping away to the centre of the earth
shimmer snakes over rocks
earthy liquid stains lips
my body beats to a different rhythm
slows its blood to cool winter
the bold placement of rocks
beauty and dust.

Eototo Studio

for Bill

In your studio the light is as soft as a stranger's breath
on the back of the neck in a crowded subway car
across the wall sketches are stretched to infinite point
a hand reaches out with the thumb turned upward
touch the crown
rack of caricatures; and I am there in red, flaming in oil
you tell me how you left your body in Flagstaff
the night your lover died
and spun out in a fractured tube of energy
into night to meet him somewhere on the plane
and came back, reluctantly, to claim your shell
you woke to find him dead on cooling cotton beside you

In your studio it is as quiet as the desert
when the noon sun spills
its energy over sand, or asphalt in the city
or the sea lilting a burnt retina black
mustang's tense jaw in blue, the angry whinny mute in metal
here it plunges and rears, clatter of silver feet on wood
the silent ones in boxes built up with dense texture
baffling sound
reflected sunset, vermilion crescents in liquid eyes
you washed his body in the still room
as day began hot and orange
secret soft skin between fingers, in all the loved crevices
smoothed damp cloth across his silent chest
around pulseless neck
dressed him in silk and laid beside him
muffling your breath, waiting

In your studio the smell of sage is as subtle
as night when it mingles
oily turpentine, tweaking it to acidity
sharpened smell tangible on hot flesh
slices of cut bronze, football player's heroic catch in hard hand
whirl abrasions swirling gold to the dissection of chest
four aspects of one movement cut through bodies
fizzing burning of metal defeating metal
knot at heart place, a plywood miniature
you breathed in the sun-warmed cherry wood of the headboard
as noon flattened shadows in the room
his cologne tight in nostrils, on your fingertips
his body softening into insistence of detergent
fragrance of laundry
flash of harsh sunlight, street noise and sirens
dry earth and the smell of regret
as you open the door to goodbye.

The End of Winter

The silver birches glow yellow against winter sky. High, empty, blue. It takes guts to stand still and absorb. Like saying you don't care about the inevitable. Let time stand still, just for a minute. There is something lush about snow melting inside your boots, socks soaking but warming to body heat. And everything warm inside clothes, the wind startling and chilling against your cheeks. Winter is ending. The melting heaviness of clean snow. River rushing hidden beneath ice. Its voice a siren to spring. Mist breathing over exhausted drifts in empty woods. The robin calling, calling. Time's sudden leap into daylight, prolonged evening sun washing the blue-pink into memory. Softening of winter-black branches. Brash fox crosses your path, looking like a small red dog. Last week a coyote was seen in the neighbourhood. In a narrow tunnel you see nothing except memories, the black walls carry the present. There is no scent, no colour, no taste on the wind. Your life accelerates, weeks over hours. The winter will end when you realize to breathe means you must stand still. One day you are trudging across invisible, weary snow. You realize your tight, hunched body aches, you have no recollection of the thousand times you have walked this path. That you don't remember your day at work or your journey home from a forced dinner last night. There is no point rushing blind toward the inevitable so you stop by the trees. Birch, golden against the blue sky, a distant white trail edging. In that moment serenity is deafening. It is frightening. The prickly nasal cavity, pupil reducing painfully and the thick throat almost forces you forward. But you stay despite the melancholy that warms deep, a memory clicking somniferous. Of warm summer gardens, heady, fragrant grasses, the red brick of an unknown building with its radiant heat. Peach juice sweet in your mouth, the touch of sun, hands on your skin. And you watch the trees, the sky, the snow and you breathe. It is the end of winter.